For you,
Happy Reading!

ISBN: 9798364116307

Growing Readers

All rights reserved

Me

T. Paris

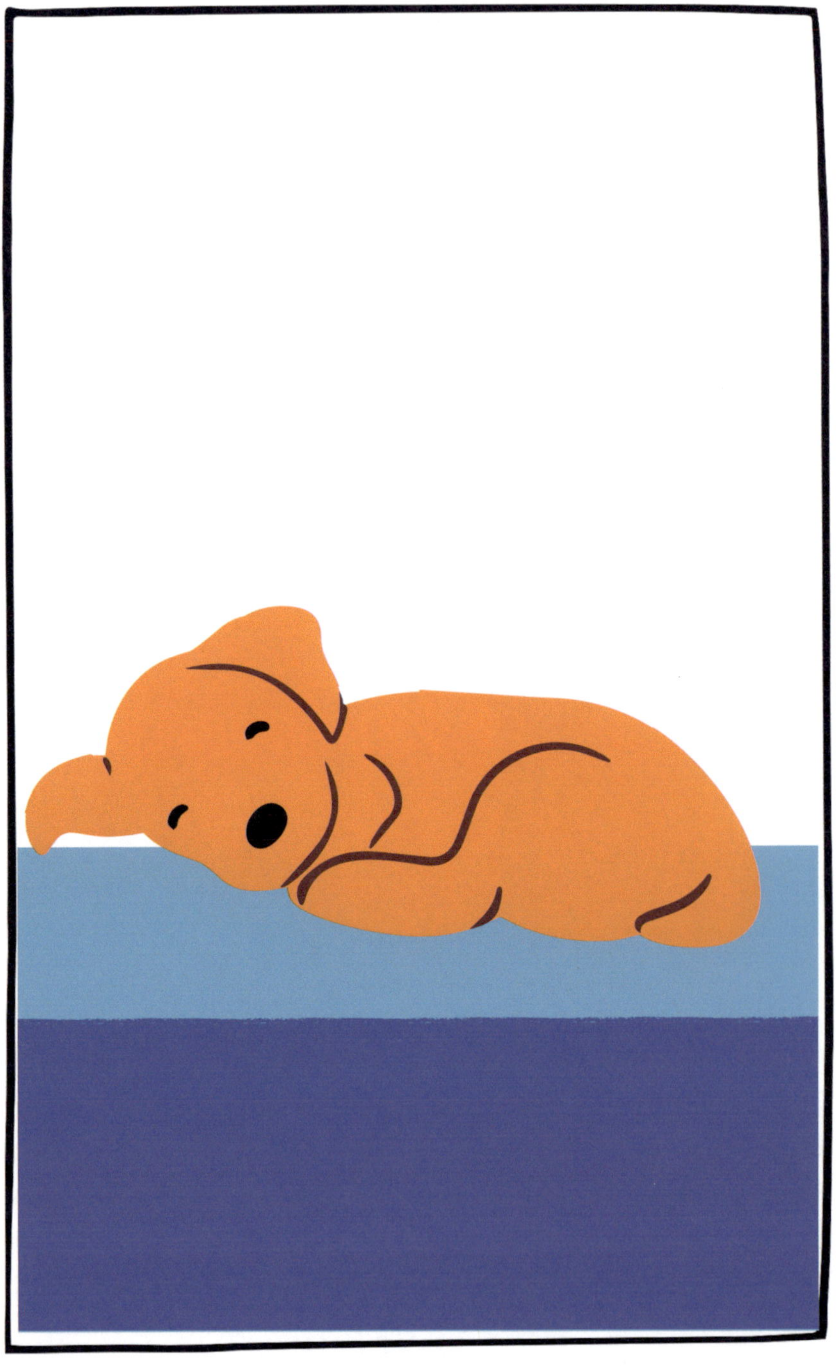

A dog

4

A car

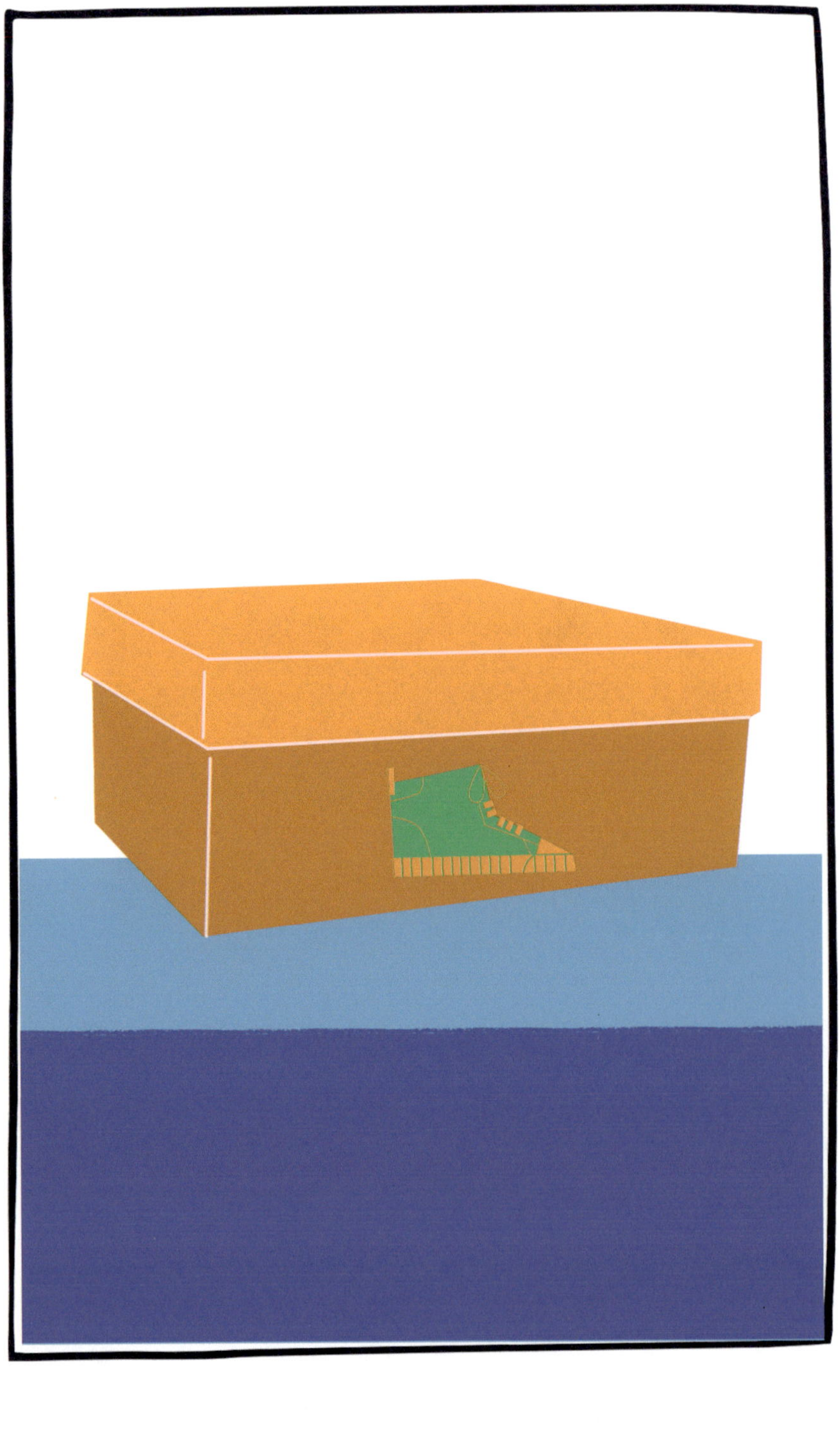

A box

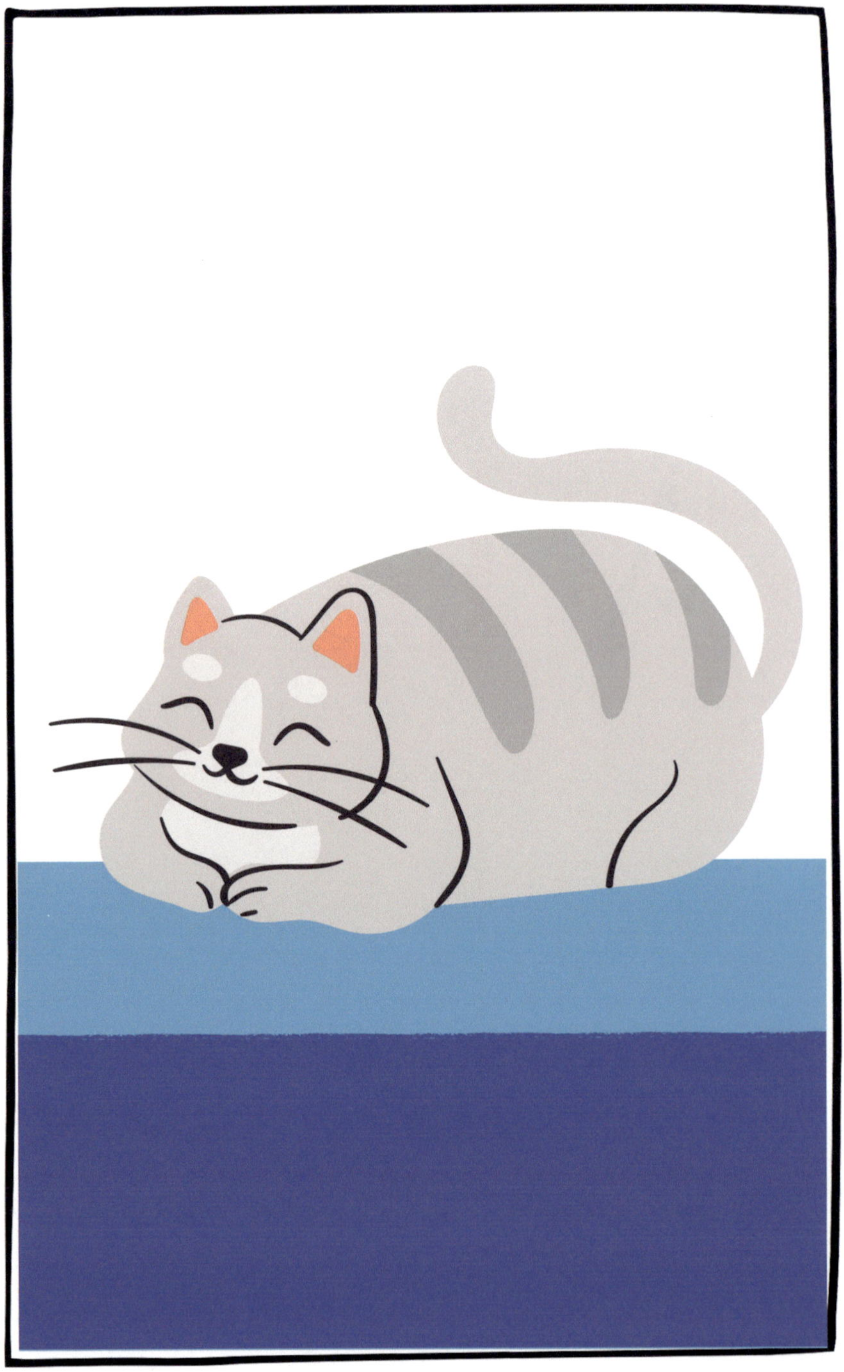

A cat

10

A pen

A mug

14

A fan

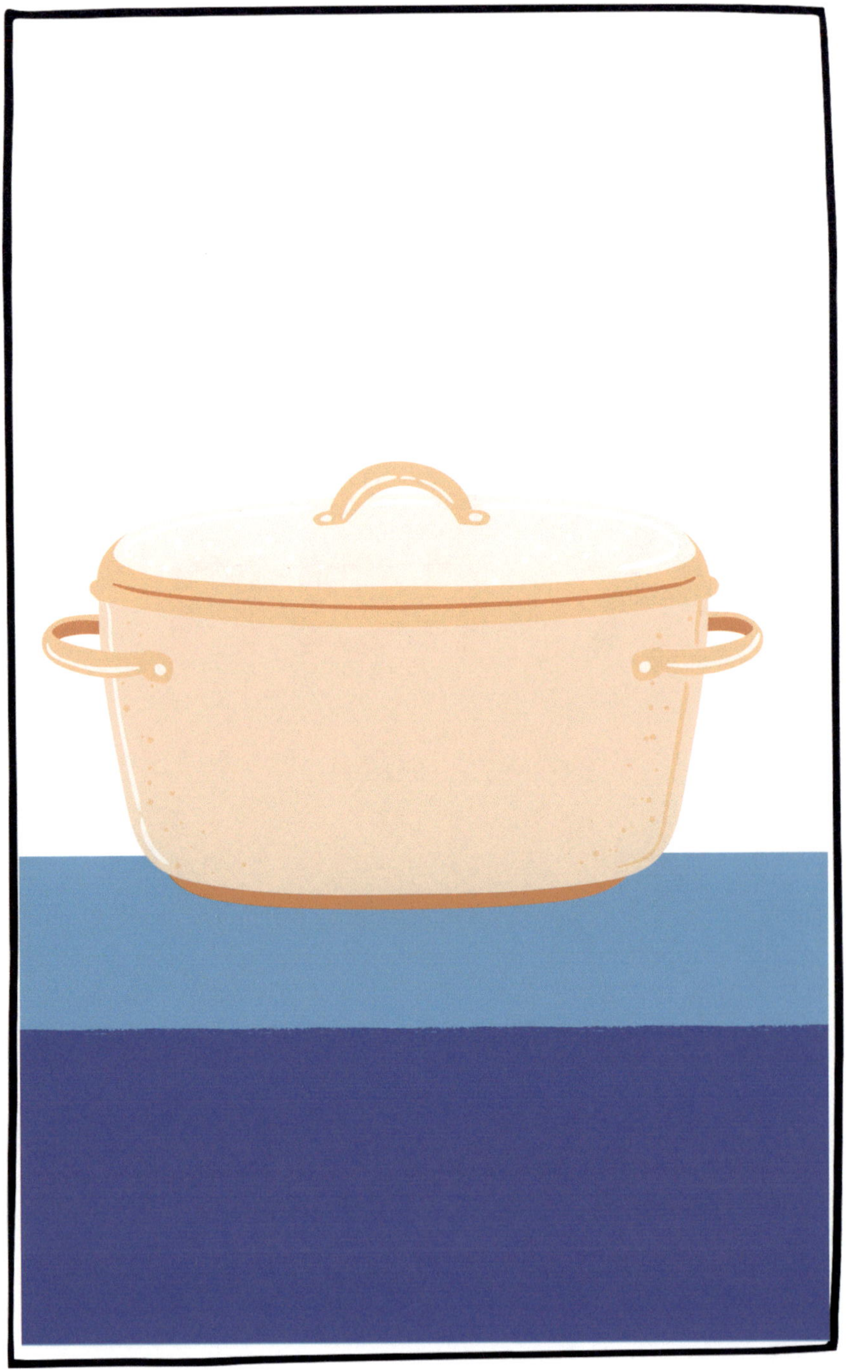

A pot

18

A fox

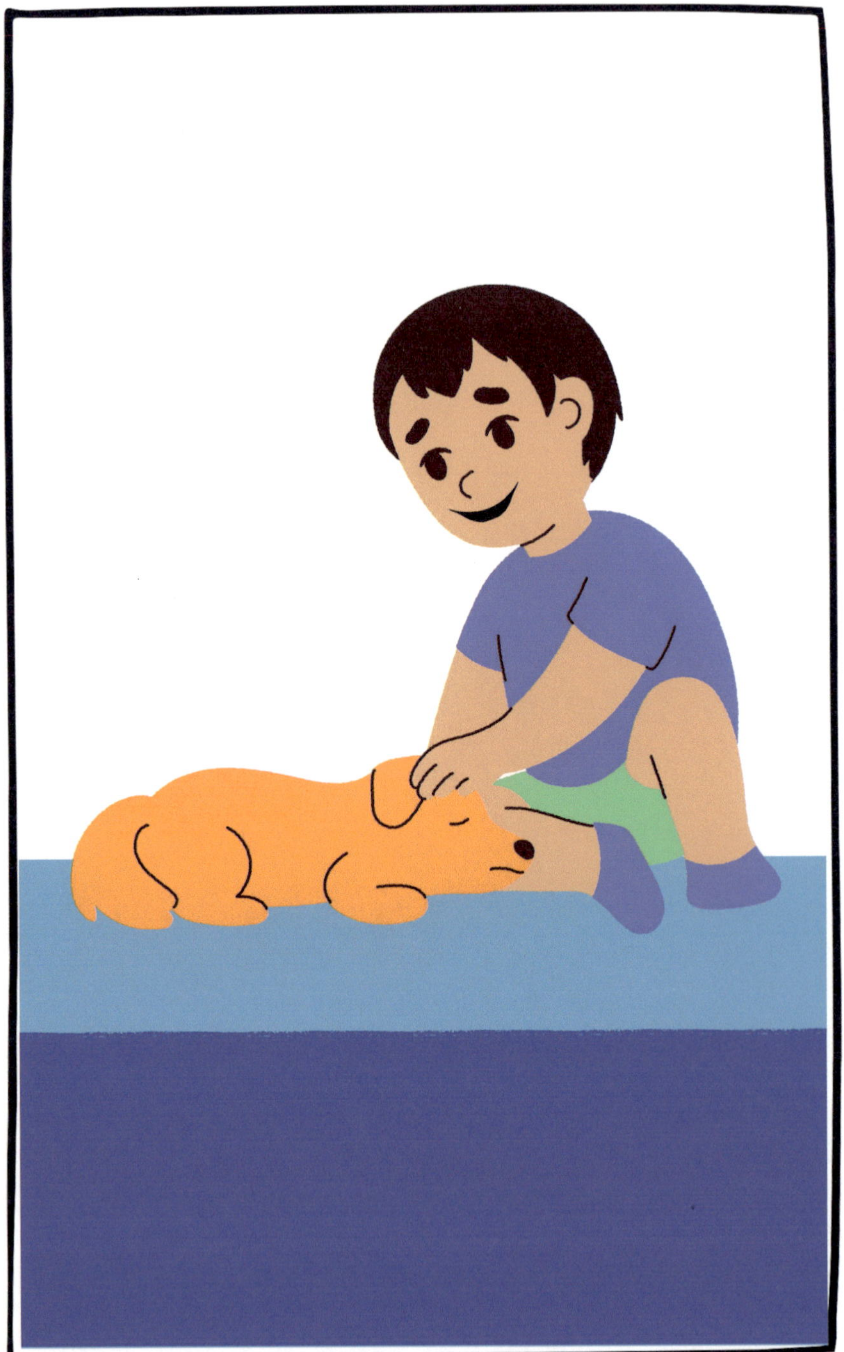

Me!

Made in the USA
Columbia, SC
05 March 2024